This book was very loved
But we needed room for new.
We hope you will enjoy it
Just as much as we did, too.

nhfpl

DIGITAL AND INFORMATION LITERACY ™

COPYRIGHT AND DIGITAL ETHICS

EMILY POPEK

rosen publishing's
rosen central

New York

Published in 2011 by The Rosen Publishing Group, Inc.
29 East 21st Street, New York, NY 10010

Copyright © 2011 by The Rosen Publishing Group, Inc.

First Edition

Library of Congress Cataloging-in-Publication Data

Popek, Emily.
Copyright and digital ethics / Emily Popek. — 1st ed.
    p. cm. — (Digital and information literacy)
Includes bibliographical references and index.
ISBN 978-1-4488-1323-0 (library binding)
ISBN 978-1-4488-2294-2 (pbk.)
ISBN 978-1-4488-2300-0 (6-pack)
1. Copyright and electronic data processing—United States.—Juvenile literature. I. Title.
KF3030.1.P67 2011
346.7304'82—dc22

                                                              2010027018

Manufactured in the United States of America

CPSIA Compliance Information: Batch #W11YA: For further information, contact Rosen Publishing, New York, New York, at 1-800-237-9932.

CONTENTS

INTRODUCTION

Open virtually any book and you will find a copyright symbol: the letter "c" with a circle around it. According to the U.S. Copyright Office, copyrights generally give an author control over how his or her creation—whether it is a book, movie, or song—will be used. The author gets to decide how and when the work can be copied, displayed, or performed. If a person or company goes against the author's wishes, that person or company may be sued or face criminal charges.

When copyright was first established by law, protecting published works was very different from what it is today. In an era when printing was a labor-intensive and skilled craft, printers could identify their original works with intricate marks or seals that were difficult to reproduce. There were fewer books produced back then, so it was much easier to identify pirated works.

Today, flatbed scanners and copy machines can create replicas of printed material, such as books, magazines, or artwork. Computers can create digital reproductions of images, music, and videos with the click of a mouse. And these reproductions can be sent around the world in a split second via the Internet. Unlike a bootleg DVD or an unauthorized copy of a book, these digital copies often leave little or no evidence of their existence, let alone their origin.

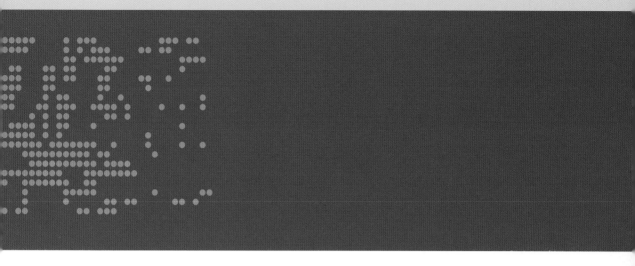

The Internet provides a unique opportunity for people to share media in ways that they never could have before. Before the Internet, there was no way for anyone, even the largest corporation in the world, to reach as many people as can be reached online today. Today, however, that power is not only available to large companies, it is also available to anyone who has access to the Internet. This ease of sharing has changed how people think about copyright protections.

Yet just because it is now incredibly easy to share a creator's music, films, books, photographs, or other kinds of art does not mean that it is right, ethical, or permissible to do so. Someone's creative work is his or her intellectual property. Sharing this property without permission or without paying for it is the same as stealing any other kind of property. Stealing someone's intellectual property—whether that involves illegal file sharing of music, cutting and pasting someone else's text into a report, or watching illegally downloaded movies—is not just unethical, it is also illegal.

Chapter 1

What Is Copyright?

n fifteenth-century Germany, a man named Johannes Gutenberg invented a printing press that made printing faster, cheaper, and easier. Before Gutenberg's invention, every letter, comma, and period that went into a book had to be cut out of a wood block by hand. Gutenberg created a system by which small individual blocks—each representing a letter, a space, or a punctuation mark—were put together to create lines of text. This was known as movable type. Gutenberg's invention made it easier for printers to produce books, and it allowed them to sell books at lower prices.

There were no copyright laws in Germany at this time, which meant a printer could reproduce virtually any printed work. Most printed works at the time were texts that had been available for centuries, such as religious texts and writings from ancient Greece.

According to Jeffrey Sun and Benjamin Baez, authors of *Intellectual Property in the Information Age*, "The first known copyrights appeared in Renaissance Italy, which granted monopolies . . . to print or sell books for a particular term." Instead of copyright, many printers operated under license,

Johannes Gutenberg's printing press was one of the first technological innovations to change the way people thought about ownership of printed materials.

which gave them the right to reproduce certain works. Once the concept of copyright was established, it spread to other nations and became law.

Copyright and You

Copyright isn't just for famous authors, musicians, and filmmakers. It's for everyone. As soon as a work is created, copyright protection becomes automatically available to the author as long as the work meets three basic conditions.

File   Edit   View   Favorites   Tools   Help

PIRACY

Piracy

In copyright law, a pirate is someone who makes unauthorized copies of a work, usually for profit. Today, it is common for computer software, movies, music, and other works to be pirated. Sometimes these copies are not always true to the original. For instance, camcording, or recording films in movie theaters, is a multimillion-dollar business. However, these recordings lack the image and sound quality of the legitimate films shown in the theater and later broadcast on television and released on DVD.

Although piracy is a violation of copyright law, some have argued that it is a "victimless crime" because making a copy doesn't stop anyone else from accessing the original if he or she chooses. But piracy can cause harm. Companies lose money when their products are pirated. As a result, they may charge consumers more money for access to their products in order to make up the money lost to piracy. In addition, any time a book, movie, song, or album is copied or shared illegally, it means that a legitimate copy of that product has gone unsold. This in turn means the artist or artists who created it do not receive the money that is due to them. So it's not only companies that are harmed; so, too, are the artists you respect and admire. If they don't receive adequate pay for their work, they may not be able to continue creating the books, music, movies, and art you love.

First, the work must be recorded in some way. A speech that is not recorded or written down can't be protected, since there is no way to reliably reproduce it. A work must also be original—it can't be something that someone else has already created. Finally, it must show at least "minimal creativity." It doesn't matter if the work is considered high quality, or if the creator ever intended to publish it or make it publicly available. As long as it meets these three criteria, it can be protected by copyright.

These last two guidelines are a bit less clear than the first. Many authors, songwriters, filmmakers, and dancers have created "original" works that are inspired by or based on the works of others. For example, the musical *West Side Story* is based on William Shakespeare's play *Romeo and Juliet*. However, *West Side Story* is not a copy of *Romeo and Juliet*. Instead, it is simply modeled on Shakespeare's play and is considered an original creative work.

It is not always obvious which works are protected by copyright. When one work is very similar to an existing work, it may be found to be infringing on the copyright of the original work. An artist may sue another if he or she believes his or her copyright has been infringed upon, but there are not usually criminal charges associated with copyright infringement.

Ntrandofende el patrone dentro la cafa doue erano quilli pulite et belli iuuenefti che auea conparate et cuffi alloro diffi. O figlioli mei piangi te la uoftra fortuna per che io fo qua con denare affai per conparare delle iumente per fareue andare ad cauallo et non donarue fatiga in della uia et non de trouo nulla per nullo denaro ad conperare ne anchora ad allo ghere ne homo ne iumenta poffo hauere per tanto quefta roba fpartitela tra uui et quifti fardelli como meglio ue parera per che domane ne uolimo partire & andare in la cita de effefi. Li ferui udito el comandamento dello patrone incomen zaro de dui in dui ad partire la roba per portarela la matina. Alli quali Efopo

Books like this one, which is a Latin retelling of the ancient Greek stories known as *Aesop's Fables*, as well as religious texts, were common during the fifteenth century and copied widely by printers.

Why Copyright?

Most historians agree that the first copyright laws were established to protect authors and printers and to ensure that the public had access to

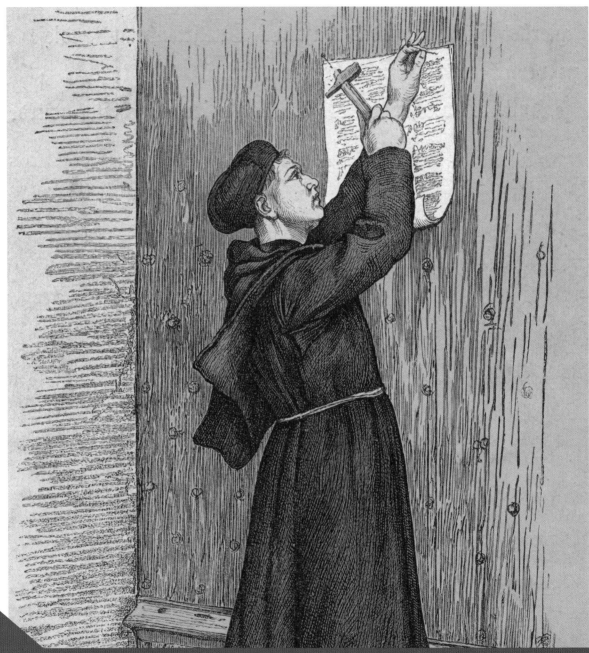

Martin Luther's published writings—including the "Ninety-Five Theses," which he is here hammering onto the door of the Castle Church in Wittenburg, Germany, in 1517—were among the most popular books of the sixteenth century.

printed materials. These concepts are still part of modern ideas about copyright.

Before there were copyright laws in Europe, some printers took advantage of books and other materials that people had worked hard to produce. Honest printers fought against "pirate" printers, who reproduced and sold the works of others without permission—and often without a great deal of accuracy.

In an essay titled "The Misunderstood Idea of Copyright," Karl-Erik Tallmo says that "piracy is historically not new. In the sixteenth century, many printers earned their entire living on pirate editions of [Martin] Luther's writings. The economic loss was, however, something that Luther regarded as a minor problem. Distorted content was a worse evil, according to him: 'Often have I had to experience that a pirated text is so incorrect that in several places I could not recognize my own work.'"

At the same time that Martin Luther was worried about people pirating his writings, others were concerned that printers' licenses gave printers too much control over written works. In 1692, British philosopher John Locke wrote to Parliament to complain about "ignorant and lazy stationers" who held licenses to classic Latin works. These printers, Locke wrote, "claim the text to be theirs, and so will not suffer fairer or more correct editions than any they print here."

TEN GREAT QUESTIONS

TO ASK A COPYRIGHT LAW EXPERT

1. Is it legal to make a mix CD to give to a friend?

2. Am I allowed to use a copyrighted image on a poster or flier?

3. Can my band perform someone else's music at a party?

4. If someone else has used my work without my permission, what should I do?

5. Does copyright law protect recipes?

6. If my class makes a movie together, who is the "author"?

7. Is my schoolwork protected by copyright?

8. How can I put my work into the public domain?

9. Can I get in trouble for linking to someone else's Web site?

10. If my friend tells me it's OK for me to use his or her work, can I do it?

Chapter 2

Copyright Law

The first American copyright laws were written in 1790 to deal with printed materials. Since then, copyright laws have changed a great deal. Many of these changes have been in response to the development of new forms of media and technology that need to be protected by copyright, such as movies, recorded music, and computer programs.

A significant difference between the first copyright laws and modern laws is the length of copyright protection. The first copyright law only protected works for a fourteen-year term that could be renewed. The first extension of the duration of copyright protection was passed in 1831. Copyright protection was extended again in 1909, 1976, and 1998. The most recent extension increased the term of copyright to the life of the author, plus seventy years.

Perhaps the most significant change since 1790 has been the making of copyright protection automatic for all qualifying works. For many years, authors, publishers, and printers had to follow certain procedures to obtain copyright protection. This included putting copyright notices on books and other publications. Today, any work that meets certain basic standards is protected by copyright as soon as it is created.

License vs. Law

Laws are not the only principles that govern how works can be used. Licenses are another tool that creators use to protect their works.

It is common to see licenses on computer software and even on Web sites. Software manufacturers often ask consumers to agree to use their software only in certain ways. For example, they may request that a person not make copies of it for family or friends, or not modify the computer program in any way. These activities might be permitted under copyright law, but if

Most computer programs ask users to agree to a license. This license specifies how the software will be used, including under what conditions the software can be copied. It is illegal to sell copies of programs such as Windows Vista, as this vendor is doing.

the user agrees to the terms of the license, he or she is legally obligated to respect and observe what the license permits and forbids. When computer owners buy a computer program, they are not actually purchasing computer programs outright. Instead, they are merely buying a license to use the programs. The programs themselves remain the intellectual property of the software company that developed them.

Some companies put licensing restrictions on media that is in the public domain. For example, the Web site iClipart.com, which sells access to royalty-free images, lists specific uses for which the images are prohibited. Many images on iClipart are in the public domain. Artists or researchers who found these public domain images on their own can do whatever they want with them, including uses prohibited by iClipart. But if the image is

By creating an artistic image of Barack Obama from a copyright-protected photograph, artist Shepard Fairey faced legal challenges to his work. Fairey has argued that his artwork constituted fair use and was not copyright infringement.

downloaded from iClipart, the person who downloaded it is bound by the terms of the license.

Copyright Goes Digital

As technologies have changed, so have copyright laws. Computer technology makes it very easy to copy music, movies, images, and text. The way that these digital copies are transmitted is different from the way that physical copies, or hard copies, are shared. This difference has posed a problem for copyright law.

Pirated DVDs, such as those held by U.S. Senator Dianne Feinstein of California, are a financial loss to the film industry. The U.S. government has enacted several laws to discourage piracy.

Before the existence of home computers, making a copy of something meant producing a physical object. Before e-books and digital scanners, a person could only share a book by loaning it to someone else. The owner of a book has the right to share, sell, or destroy it. However, if an individual or company were to make a copy of the book and try to sell it, that would be a violation of copyright.

File   Edit   View   Favorites   Tools   Help

AMERICAN AND FOREIGN COPYRIGHT LAWS

American and Foreign Copyright Laws

In the 1800s, copyright laws were still a new concept around the world, and different countries had very different laws. This caused problems between nations. In the United States, the works of British authors were not given copyright protection. This hurt both nations, as Siva Vaidhyanathan explains in his book *Copyrights and Copywrongs*: "British books sold at a much lower price in the United States than American-written books did, but British authors saw no return from the pirated editions. British authors felt stiffed, and American books could not compete with cheaper British works." To correct this, the two nations signed an agreement in 1891 that protected each other's authors.

Several nations signed the Berne Convention for the Protection of Literary and Artistic Works in 1886 in Berne, Switzerland. The basic principle of the Berne Convention is that each country grants the same copyright protection to foreign works as it does for its own works. It sets a minimum term for the protection of works—fifty years after the death of the author—but allows countries to set longer terms if they want.

The United States did not join the Berne Convention until more than one hundred years later, in 1989, because the terms were so different from U.S. copyright laws. As of 2008, 164 countries were party to the Berne Convention. Its terms have been revised many times since 1886.

In the digital world, it is very hard to share something without making a copy of it. And since making a copy of a copyright-protected work is illegal, this makes things complicated. Online, there is no difference between reading and copying—you can't do one without the other. When someone visits a news Web site to read a news story, his or her computer makes a copy of that story and displays it on the computer screen. Another copy of the story is created if the reader hits the site's "e-mail this story" button and sends the story to a friend.

This is a harmless, legitimate, and acceptable form of copying. Yet the Internet is also used to sell or give away illegal copies of music, text, and images. When this first began happening, copyright holders started asking

Far from being a "victimless crime," piracy can hurt the movie industry, as it has in Lebanon. Recently, the Lebanese government destroyed hundreds of thousands of pirated DVDs and reported that more than half of the media sold in that country are illegal copies of copyrighted work.

for stricter laws to protect their works. In the 1990s, American lawmakers began rewriting copyright law to include computers and the Internet. Congress passed the Digital Millennium Copyright Act (DMCA) in 1998. According to the University of California at Los Angeles Online Institute for Cyberspace Law and Policy, the central goal of this act is to stop the piracy of music, films, and computer software. However, it also includes several other provisions.

One of the most lasting impacts of the DMCA has been what is called the "safe harbor" provision. The safe harbor concept means that the people in charge of hosting Web sites are not responsible for copyright-protected content on their sites if someone who visits the site puts it there. However, if the site's Webmasters are asked to take the content down by the copyright owner of the posted material, they must do so. This provision has allowed Web sites such as YouTube, Flickr, and Facebook to prosper despite the fact that their users routinely post copyright-protected music and images on these sites.

At the same time, the DMCA made it illegal for consumers to find ways around mechanisms designed to prohibit the copying of software, DVDs, or CDs. Before the act, copyright law generally allowed consumers to make copies for personal, noncommercial use (such as someone recording music onto a cassette tape). The act changed that. Most video and audio recordings available today have a Content Scramble System, or CSS. Any mechanism for breaking the CSS is illegal under the DMCA. This means that it is technically illegal to rip CDs or DVDs and put them on an MP3 player or store a copy on a home computer. Many people have argued that this part of the act goes against the principle of fair use, which will be defined in the next chapter.

Chapter 3

Using and Citing Works

Most of the material that a student will come across when doing research—Web sites and books, magazines, newspapers, and other printed material, not to mention audio and video files— is protected by copyright. Students can make use of any material, whether it is protected by copyright or not, as long as they follow the correct citation procedure.

The most important principle is giving credit where credit is due. Most scholars agree that as long as content is properly cited, it is permissible for students to make reference to, and even quote, copyright-protected works.

Plagiarism, or taking credit for someone else's work, is a serious matter. Not only is this unethical and dishonest, but it can also get a student into a lot of trouble. Plagiarism doesn't simply refer to the copying and use of someone else's words. It also refers to the copying and use of someone else's ideas, or what is known as intellectual property. While ideas are not protected by copyright, it is considered plagiarism if someone takes credit for an idea that is not his or her own. That idea is someone else's intellectual property— something that originated with that person and belongs to that person.

Steven Vander Ark, author of *The Harry Potter Lexicon*, had to alter his book after his publisher was sued by J. K. Rowling, author of the Harry Potter books, for copyright infringement. A judge ruled that Vander Ark used too much of Rowling's work to be considered original.

Plagiarism is not considered a violation of criminal law. It won't result in jail time. But it is a violation of civil law and can result in ruinously expensive lawsuits. While plagiarism is not criminally illegal, unauthorized use of copyrighted works is. If a newspaper publishes an article that someone else wrote for another publication, this could violate copyright law.

In an article titled "Plagiarism: How to Avoid It," Alexandra Babione recommends that students give credit when citing facts, dates, and other information; incorporating other people's theories, opinions, and beliefs into their original work; using exact quotes; and paraphrasing information.

Fair Use

Fair use is an exception to the protections of copyright in certain situations. For instance, book, movie, and music reviews often quote the material being reviewed. As long as the quotations are not extremely long, this is usually considered fair use. Academic research is another situation in which material can be used or quoted without infringing on copyright. Fair use must produce something new, rather than just creating a copy. And all sources must be clearly cited.

Students' work is not likely to be the subject of a lawsuit the way a popular song or movie might be. But students must adhere to the same standards as published authors. No matter what the situation, it is not right to use someone else's work without following the appropriate procedures.

The Public Domain

Not everything is protected by copyright. Copyright protections are limited to a certain period of time. Today in the United States, most copyrights last for the author's life, plus seventy years. Because copyrights expire, there are thousands of works that are no longer protected by copyright. These works are considered part of the public domain, which means that they can be freely used by anyone without restriction.

File   Edit   View   Favorites   Tools   Help

      PARODY

Parody

Parodies are a well-known example of fair use. A parody is a humorous version of something, such as a song, poem, or story. Parodies have a long history in literature, stretching as far back as ancient Greece. In modern times, parodies have been popular in film, television, magazines, and music.

One famous parodist is "Weird Al" Yankovic. Beginning in the 1980s, the entertainer has made a career of recording parodies of famous songs. Even though his songs were nearly identical in musical terms to original recordings by Michael Jackson, Nirvana, and other artists, Yankovic was able to release these songs with different and humorous lyrics without getting in trouble. Courts have usually allowed this sort of copying because it is necessary to make some reference to an original work in order to comment on it in a funny way. By writing new lyrics to existing melodies, Yankovic wasn't merely copying other people's work but creating new songs with new meanings.

"Weird Al" Yankovic became famous for parodies of popular songs beginning in the 1980s. Despite legal challenges, Yankovic has put out numerous albums parodying popular music hits.

Many classic works of literature, including the writings of Shakespeare, Jane Austen, and Charles Dickens, are in the public domain. Publishers can print copies of these books without paying the authors' families or estates. Directors can create plays and movies based on these authors'

The works of William Shakespeare are in the public domain, making performances, such as this production of his play *Twelfth Night*, possible without any need to ask for permission.

stories without asking permission. Authors can quote lines from these works without citation.

The 1709 Statute of Anne in Great Britain put the idea of public domain into law. The government felt it was reasonable that authors and printers should be able to profit from their work, but only for a limited time. Even though copyright laws have changed over the years, public domain is still an important concept. However, there is a great deal of debate about the issue. Many people believe that the copyright terms have become too long and should be shorter—or not exist at all. Others believe that copyright should last longer, or it should be easier to renew.

Reinventing the Commons

Many groups and individuals say copyright laws should be less restrictive and allow the public to have more freedom. They argue that copyright laws are too favorable to the copyright holder. This belief is integral to the copyleft movement.

"Copyleft" is a play on the word "copyright," suggesting a more liberal, or left-wing, approach to copyright. The copyleft movement includes people who argue that all content should be completely free of restrictions, as well as those who believe copyright law should be modified or reformed but not abolished altogether.

Computer programmers have often been advocates for more freedom from copyright restrictions. In 1983, a computer software developer named Richard Stallman announced his plan to create a software system called GNU that would be completely free for users to "run, copy, distribute, study, change, and improve."

In 1985, Stallman founded the Free Software Foundation, which became an advocacy organization for the free software movement. The foundation's licenses for software and other works offer more freedom than traditional copyright does. The online encyclopedia Wikipedia, which allows any user to add or edit its content, is one of the best-known examples of a Web site that uses a GNU Free Documentation License.

Stallman was not alone in his belief that users should have the ability to improve and modify software. Many computer hackers—people who modify existing software or gain illegal access to computer systems—believe that computer software should be openly available to all. In 1998, a group

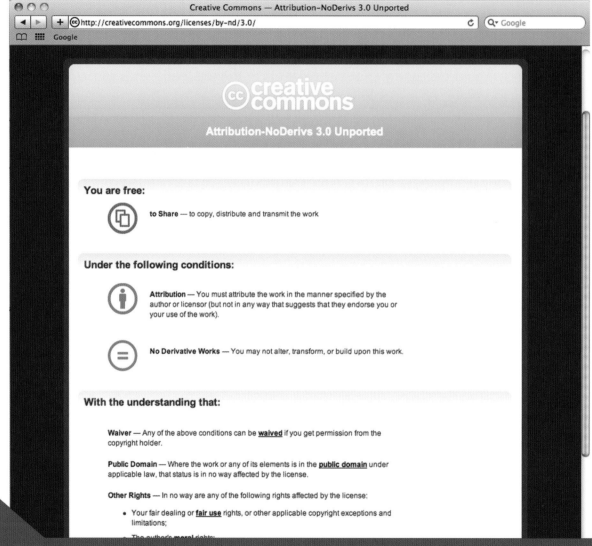

The various licenses offered by Creative Commons (http://www.creativecommons.org) spell out the conditions for use of a given work. Some have argued, however, that it is difficult to enforce the terms of these licenses.

of people with roots in the computer hacker community got together to promote the idea of open source software—software that users can redistribute, modify, and study freely. They founded the Open Source Initiative, which issues licenses for software that meets these standards.

Creative Commons, founded in 2002, also issues licenses. Its licenses are designed for writing, art, photography, music, film, Web sites, and similar works. The organization offers several different types of licenses, each with its own conditions. Some have criticized the variety of Creative Commons licenses, calling them confusing. They also point out that Creative Commons licenses are not enforceable under the laws of certain countries. Others have praised the organization for offering users a range of choices regarding how their work will be used.

All of these types of licenses give artists, writers, and others ways of sharing their work while still retaining some of the protections of copyright. Licenses such as these are necessary because of the automatic copyright protection afforded to all recorded works that meet the basic standards of originality and creativity.

Chapter 4

Digital Etiquette

Many people understand that bringing a video camera into a movie theater and recording the film is a copyright infringement. But those same people do not always recognize that copying a picture from somewhere on the Web and posting it on their own Web site is equally wrong.

Copyright laws do not discriminate in favor of or against the Internet. A photograph taken with film and reproduced on paper has the same protections as one taken with a digital camera and uploaded to a Web site. The same is true for music, movies, and other works created and distributed by either traditional or digital means. However, by following fair use guidelines and identifying works that are licensed for broader use or are in the public domain, students can find and freely use a wealth of online material.

Navigating the Commons

Many organizations provide access to works in the public domain. These organizations ensure the legality of using and reproducing these works so that users don't have to worry about violating copyright law.

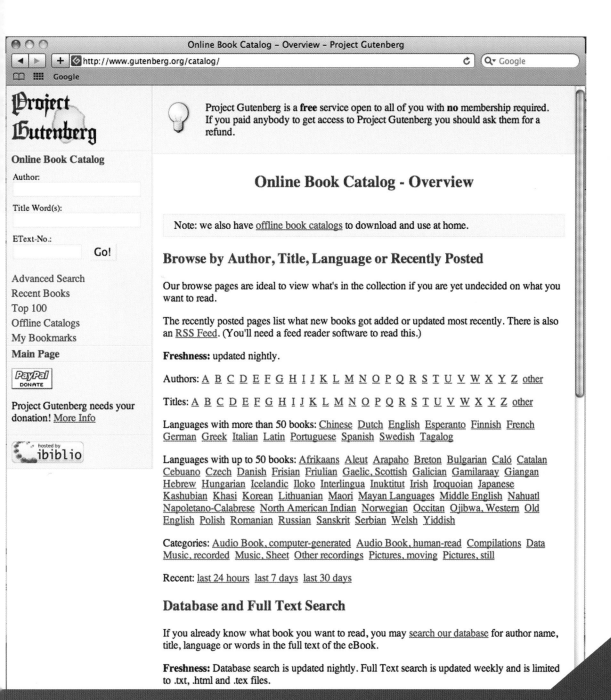

○ ○ ○   Online Book Catalog – Overview – Project Gutenberg

◄ ► + 🌐 http://www.gutenberg.org/catalog/   ℃   Q▾ Google

📖 ▦   Google

Project Gutenberg

Online Book Catalog

Author:

Title Word(s):

EText-No.:

[   ] **Go!**

Advanced Search
Recent Books
Top 100
Offline Catalogs
My Bookmarks
Main Page

PayPal DONATE

Project Gutenberg needs your donation! More Info

🐾 hosted by ibiblio

💡 Project Gutenberg is a **free** service open to all of you with **no** membership required. If you paid anybody to get access to Project Gutenberg you should ask them for a refund.

Online Book Catalog - Overview

Note: we also have offline book catalogs to download and use at home.

Browse by Author, Title, Language or Recently Posted

Our browse pages are ideal to view what's in the collection if you are yet undecided on what you want to read.

The recently posted pages list what new books got added or updated most recently. There is also an RSS Feed. (You'll need a feed reader software to read this.)

Freshness: updated nightly.

Authors: A B C D E F G H I J K L M N O P Q R S T U V W X Y Z other

Titles: A B C D E F G H I J K L M N O P Q R S T U V W X Y Z other

Languages with more than 50 books: Chinese Dutch English Esperanto Finnish French German Greek Italian Latin Portuguese Spanish Swedish Tagalog

Languages with up to 50 books: Afrikaans Aleut Arapaho Breton Bulgarian Caló Catalan Cebuano Czech Danish Frisian Friulian Gaelic, Scottish Galician Gamilaraay Giangan Hebrew Hungarian Icelandic Iloko Interlingua Inuktitut Irish Iroquoian Japanese Kashubian Khasi Korean Lithuanian Maori Mayan Languages Middle English Nahuatl Napoletano-Calabrese North American Indian Norwegian Occitan Ojibwa, Western Old English Polish Romanian Russian Sanskrit Serbian Welsh Yiddish

Categories: Audio Book, computer-generated Audio Book, human-read Compilations Data Music, recorded Music, Sheet Other recordings Pictures, moving Pictures, still

Recent: last 24 hours last 7 days last 30 days

Database and Full Text Search

If you already know what book you want to read, you may search our database for author name, title, language or words in the full text of the eBook.

Freshness: Database search is updated nightly. Full Text search is updated weekly and is limited to .txt, .html and .tex files.

Web sites such as Project Gutenberg (http://www.gutenberg.org) conduct research to ensure that the texts they offer are in the public domain and not protected by copyright.

Project Gutenberg (http://www.gutenberg.org) is an organization devoted to offering free electronic books online. The majority of the thousands of books available through Project Gutenberg are in the public domain in the United States. Others are governed by licenses, which detail the terms of use.

Woman aircraft worker, Vega Aircraft Corporation, Burbank, Calif. Shown checking electrical assemblies (LOC)

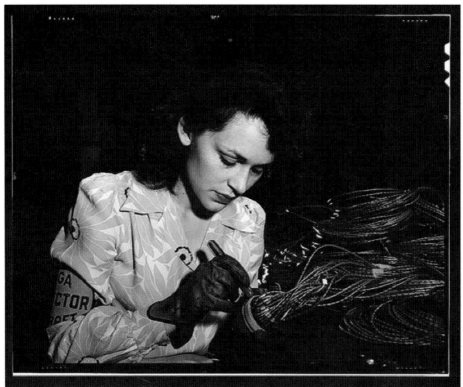

Bransby, David,, photographer.

Text isn't the only public domain material available online. Images, such as this one from the Library of Congress's photo stream on Flickr (http://www.flickr.com/photos/library_of_congress), are also available for anyone to use.

A similar organization, iBiblio, describes itself as "a conservancy of freely available information, including software, music, literature, art, history, science, politics, and cultural studies." Its Web site (http://www.ibiblio.org) contains images, text files, music, and videos. Like Wikipedia, the database is user-generated. While not all the works listed on iBiblio are in the public domain, many are licensed through Creative Commons for various uses.

The photo-sharing Web site Flickr has its own commons, which features photographs in the public domain provided by organizations such as the Library of Congress, Smithsonian Museum, New York Public Library, and U.S. National Archives. Materials from Sweden, Australia, England,

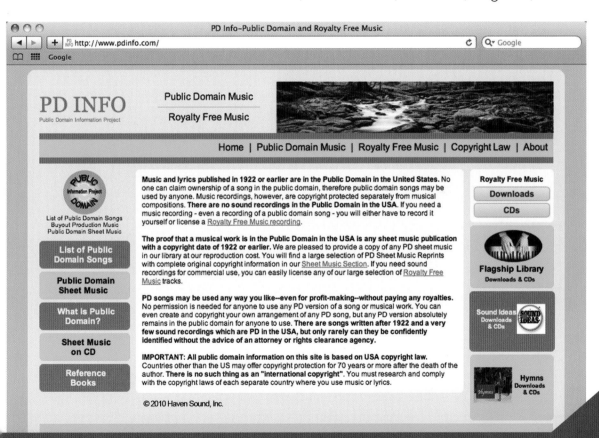

Web sites such as the Public Domain Information Project (http://www.pdinfo.com) help users determine what songs are in the public domain. However, public-domain status may not apply to specific recordings of those songs, which can still be protected by copyright.

Scotland, New Zealand, and France are also included. The database includes artwork as well as photographs.

The Public Domain Information Project (http://www.pdinfo.com) has a searchable database of music that has entered the public domain. Anyone is free to perform, record, rewrite, adapt, or quote from these works. It is important to note, as the Web site points out, that only the music itself is in the public domain—not necessarily any recordings of that music.

Since only works published before 1923 are automatically in the public domain, there are very few well-known films in this category. However, some films have come into the public domain because the copyright holder failed to renew the copyright—something that was necessary for much of the twentieth century.

Protected or Not?

It can be notoriously tricky to tell for sure if something is protected by copyright or not. As Steven Fishman, author of *The Public Domain: How to Find & Use Copyright-Free Writings, Music, Art & More*, explains, "Public domain materials don't look any different than works still protected by copyright. The fact that a work contains a copyright notice—the [copyright symbol] followed by the publication name and date—does not necessarily mean it really is protected by copyright law."

Students should proceed as if the works they encounter are protected by copyright unless they have a clear reason to believe otherwise. This is hard enough with books, music, and movies, but it can be even harder online. While most commercial Web sites will contain some sort of copyright notice, personal Web sites such as blogs may not.

Creative Commons licenses are often used for images, sound recordings, movies, or entire Web sites. Students should look for the symbol, the letters "CC" in an oval-shaped outline, to indicate a Creative Commons license. However, it is important to remember that, especially on the Web, the absence of a copyright or Creative Commons symbol does not mean the work is in the public domain.

File sharing of music is a hotly debated issue. Some, like Michael Petricone *(above center)* of the Consumer Electronic Association, believe people should have more freedom to share files. Others believe file sharing effectively robs artists and content creators of money they are owed.

File Sharing

File sharing is one of the most controversial issues in copyright and fair use. There are many Web sites and computer programs designed to allow users to share files, such as songs, videos, and software.

For many years, it was not considered illegal for one person to share a copy of a song or video with a friend. This was protected as fair use as long as the copy was given freely and not sold. The Internet and the

DMCA changed that. Record companies and film studios became more worried about copying when the Internet gave millions of people access to copies of popular music and movies. The DMCA made it illegal to copy and share these files.

It may ease one's conscience to think that everyone participates in file sharing, or that it is easy to get away with. Neither of these beliefs is true, however. The Recording Industry Association of America has filed hundreds of lawsuits against regular people—housewives, college students, young children, and grandparents—for sharing files or owning illegal copies of music. Some of these people had thousands of illegal files; others had only a few. Many of these people received no warning before they were sued for thousands of dollars.

Not only is file sharing illegal in most instances, but many people also believe that it is unethical. While some artists make their work available at no charge, most music, films, and computer software is protected by copyright. Creating or obtaining an unauthorized copy of a protected work takes something away from the person or group that created the work.

When copyright was first introduced, it was essentially a bargain struck between those who produce works (such as writers, artists, and composers) and their audience. The protections of copyright gave artists a reason to continue creating new works. By protecting these works from piracy and ensuring that the producer could have some control over how the content reached the audience, it was believed that creativity would be encouraged. Without such encouragement, it was believed that art and literature would cease to exist. Creating or obtaining unauthorized copies of copyright-protected works violates the implicit agreement between the artist and the audience.

User-Generated Content

Many popular Web sites, including YouTube, Flickr, and Facebook, consist mainly of what is called user-generated content. The photos, videos, and text on these sites were put there not by Webmasters but by users—Web site

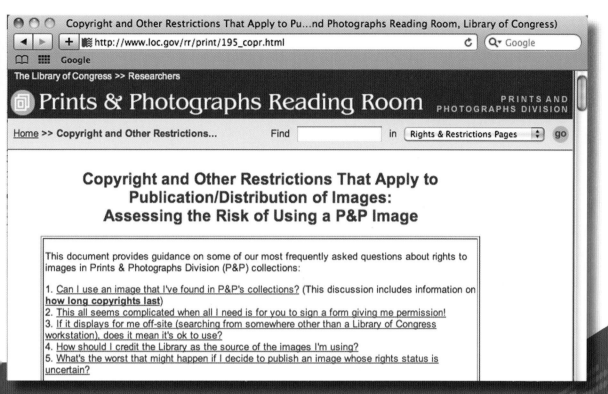

Copyright and reproduction rights associated with images are complicated issues, as this screen shot from the Library of Congress (http://www.loc.gov) illustrates. If there is any possibility a work might be protected by copyright, it is safest not to use it if you have not sought and received explicit permission to do so.

visitors who have created an account and posted images, videos, and text. Identifying copyrights for user-generated content can be very difficult. Many people post other peoples' material (such as film clips, art, or songs) without permission to do so. This is a violation of copyright law and can put the poster at risk for legal action.

Others may create original works derived from, or using parts of, copyright-protected works. Sometimes this is considered illegal; other times, it is considered fair use. There are no clear guidelines about which is which. With user-generated content, it is best to assume, as with anything, that the works are protected by copyright unless it is explicitly stated that they are not.

File　Edit　View　Favorites　Tools　Help

PROTECTING YOUR WORK

Protecting Your Work

Users who post their own videos, photos, or songs online can do so know-ing that their work is protected by copyright. However, that protection may not always be respected. Putting works online makes them available to a very wide audience, including those who may want to copy those works without asking permission. Users who don't mind having their work repub-lished, altered, or used for commercial purposes should label it accordingly, either with a Creative Commons license or some other clear statement. It is important to carefully consider the pros and cons of such a license.

Once a person has granted these uses of a work, that person can't change his or her mind and take those rights back. As the Creative Commons Web site explains, "You cannot stop someone, who has obtained your work under a Creative Commons license, from using the work according to that license. You can stop offering your work under a Creative Commons license at any time you wish; but this will not affect the rights associated with any copies of your work already in circulation under a Creative Commons license."

If a user finds that his or her work has been used without permission, there are several things that he or she can do. The first step should be to contact the individual or organization responsible for the unauthorized use of the work to tell them they do not have permission to use it. The next step would be to hire a lawyer and file a civil lawsuit against the infringing party.

When either posting content to a Web site or downloading content from a Web site, it is important to read and understand the site's terms of use. Most Web sites, including those mentioned above, specifically pro-hibit the use of any copyright-protected works. It is not hard to find content on these sites that was posted illegally. It is best to use common sense and remember that just because something can be found online doesn't necessarily mean that it is free for anyone to use.

Whether sources are found online or in more traditional hard-copy archives (like libraries), it is important to give credit when using other people's works. In an academic setting, students should credit the works they used during research—digital and traditionally published—so that the teacher can evaluate their work. Just because a source is found on the Internet doesn't mean it doesn't have to be cited properly. Not giving proper credit for an image, song, or video used in one's report, presentation, blog posting, or Web site could lead to legal action.

Since determining copyright status is so difficult, the safest way to use someone else's online work is to post a link to it, rather than reposting the work itself. While it is generally accepted that short quotes from printed material are allowed under fair use, the same rule does not always apply to short clips of music or video. Users who want permission to reproduce an image, song, or video should try to determine who holds the copyright and ask for permission to use the work. Be as specific as possible about the intended use when seeking permission.

Conclusion

Copyright is a very complicated field of law. It is best to start from the assumption that a work is protected by copyright—not only because of the difficulty of researching copyright status, but also out of respect for the work's creator. The rules governing fair use are not always clear and thus are open to interpretation.

The DMCA changed the definition of fair use to exclude most digital media, including certain CDs, DVDs, and computer software. There are organizations and individuals who argue that the DMCA has had negative and unintended consequences. Yet until the law is changed, it remains illegal to copy these media, even for personal use. While many people do not obey this law, it is important to remember that disobeying the law can lead to expensive lawsuits and possible criminal charges.

Legal issues aren't the only reason it is important to give credit for other people's words and ideas. Doing so is a meaningful way for students to demonstrate they have done their research properly.

Students should not be guided just by the letter of the law. There is a long and important tradition of scholars acknowledging the work of others. Students should consider themselves part of this proud and honorable tradition. As Alexandra Babione put it, "When you acknowledge that someone else has thought as you do, you provide support for your ideas and opinions."

Copyright laws may evolve to keep pace with the times, but they will never be obsolete. By acknowledging the sources of their research, inspiration, and ideas, students place themselves in a tradition of scholarship that stretches back for centuries. They demonstrate to their teachers that they know how to conduct research appropriately. Most important, they ensure that they have not infringed on the copyright of any of the works they reference.

MYTHS&FACTS

MYTH Copyrights have to be granted to an author by the U.S. Copyright Office.

FACT Copyright protections are afforded to all unique works—music, movies, essays, stories, etc.—even if the author doesn't register the work with the Copyright Office. Authors can also register their work with Creative Commons.

MYTH Only a direct quote or exact copy is considered copyright infringement.

FACT Something that is substantially similar—though not identical—to the original can still be considered a violation of copyright protection. If a writer passes off someone else's original work as his or her own, it's not only a violation of copyright, but it's also plagiarism. Students who are unsure of whether or not to cite something should speak with their school librarian.

MYTH Putting something on the Internet automatically places it in the public domain.

FACT While it is true that public domain works can be found on the Internet, the act of publishing something online doesn't alter its copyright status in any way. Most works found online, including videos, music, and text, are protected by copyright and should not be copied or used without permission.

GLOSSARY

charge A formal statement of wrongdoing or criminal activity. A charge is only an accusation; the accused is innocent until found guilty.

cite A reference to another source, or the act of referencing a source.

copyright The legal right to control a work for a specific period of time.

fair use The conditions under which copyright-protected works can be used without permission of the copyright holder.

infringe To violate or go against another's rights.

lawsuit A legal proceeding where one party brings an action against another. Often shortened to "suit."

license A legal document giving permission to do something.

media The plural of "medium"; the materials used to create something; also used to refer to news-gathering organizations.

monopoly Exclusive control or possession of something.

piracy The unauthorized reproduction of copyrighted materials.

plagiarize To take credit for work created by someone else.

public domain Works that are not protected by copyright.

replica A reproduction or copy.

statute A law or an act of government.

FOR MORE INFORMATION

Canadian Motion Picture Distributors Association
55 St. Clair Avenue West, Suite 210
Toronto, ON M4V 2Y7
Canada
(416) 961-1888
Web site: http://www.cmpda.ca
The Canadian Motion Picture Distributors Association is an organization that
    serves Canadian television and film companies. Its Web site includes
    information about movie and television piracy.

The Copyright Society of the USA
352 Seventh Avenue, Suite 739
New York, NY 10001
Web site: http://www.csusa.org
The Copyright Society is an organization that works to advance copyright law.

Media Awareness Network
1500 Merivale Road, 3rd Floor
Ottawa, ON K2E 6Z5
Canada
(613) 224-7721
Web site: http://www.media-awareness.ca
The Media Awareness Network is a nonprofit organization that provides
    information about young people and the media, including the Internet.

Purdue Online Writing Lab
Heavilon Hall 226
Purdue University
West Lafayette, IN 47907

(765) 494-3723
Web site: http://owl.english.purdue.edu
The Purdue Online Writing Lab includes information for students about citing
    works, avoiding plagiarism, and conducting research.

Recording Industry Association of America
1025 F Street NW, 10th Floor
Washington, DC 20004
(202) 775-0101
Web site: http://www.riaa.org
The Recording Industry Association of America provides research tools for
    students, parents, and teachers to learn more about digital music, file
    sharing, and piracy.

U.S. Copyright Office
101 Independence Avenue SE
Washington, DC 20559-6000
(202) 707-3000
Web site: http://www.copyright.gov
The U.S. Copyright Office provides copyright registration for a variety of
    works. Its records can be searched online or in person.

Web Sites

Due to the changing nature of Internet links, Rosen Publishing has developed
an online list of Web sites related to the subject of this book. This site is
updated regularly. Please use this link to access the list:

http://www.rosenlinks.com/dil/cde

Aoki, Keith, and James Boyle. *Bound by Law?: Tales from the Public Domain*. Chapel Hill, NC: Duke University Press, 2008.

Demers, Joanna, and Rosemary Coombe. *Steal This Music: How Intellectual Property Law Affects Musical Creativity*. Athens, GA: University of Georgia Press, 2006.

Engdahl, Sylvia. *Cybercrime* (Issues on Trial). Chicago, IL: Greenhaven Press, 2006.

Espejo, Roman. *Copyright Infringement* (Opposing Viewpoints). Chicago, IL: Greenhaven Press, 2009.

Fishman, Stephen. *The Copyright Handbook: What Every Writer Needs to Know*. Berkeley, CA: Nolo, 2008.

Fisk, Nathan W. *Understanding Online Piracy: The Truth About Illegal File Sharing*. Santa Barbara, CA: ABC-CLIO, 2009.

Hudson, David L., Jr. *Protecting Ideas* (Point/Counterpoint). New York, NY: Chelsea House, 2005.

LaFrance, Mary. *Copyright Law in a Nutshell*. Eagen, MN: West, 2008.

Riley, Gail. *Internet Piracy* (Controversy!). Salt Lake City, UT: Benchmark Books, 2010.

Rimmer, Matthew. *Digital Copyright and the Consumer Revolution: Hands Off My iPod*. Cheltenham, England: Edward Elgar Publishing, 2007.

Simpson, Carol. *Copyright for Schools*. Worthington, OH: Linworth Publishing, 2005.

Torr, James D., and Helen Conrath. *Internet Piracy* (At Issue). Chicago, IL: Greenhaven Press, 2007.

Waxer, Barbara, and Marsha Baum. *Copyright on the Internet: Illustrated Essentials*. Independence, KY: Course Technology, 2006.

Wilson, Lee. *Fair Use, Free Use, and Use by Permission*. New York, NY: Allworth Press, 2005.

BIBLIOGRAPHY

Broussard, Sharee L. "The Copyleft Movement: Creative Commons Licensing." *Communication Research Trends*, September 2007. Retrieved March 30, 2010 (http://findarticles.com/p/articles/ mi_7081/is_3_26/ai_n28457434).

Dautrich, Kenneth, David A. Yalof, and Mark Hugo Lopez. *The Future of the First Amendment: The Digital Media, Civic Education, and Free Expression Rights in America's High Schools.* Lanham, MD: Rowman & Littlefield, 2008.

Deane, Daniella. "Out of the Theater, Into the Courtroom: Brief Taping Brings Charges." *Washington Post*, August 1, 2007. Retrieved April 9, 2010 (http://www.washingtonpost.com/wp-dyn/content/article/ 2007/08/01/AR2007080102398.html).

Fishman, Stephen. *The Public Domain: How to Find & Use Copyright-Free Writings, Music, Art & More.* Berkeley, CA: Nolo, 2006.

Hirtle, Peter B. "Copyright Term and the Public Domain in the United States." Cornell Copyright Information Center, 2010. Retrieved March 23, 2010 (http://www.copyright.cornell.edu/resources/ publicdomain.cfm).

Lathrop, Ann, and Kathleen Foss, eds. *Guiding Students from Cheating and Plagiarism to Honesty and Integrity: Strategies for Change.* Westport, CT: Libraries Unlimited, 2005.

Lessig, Lawrence. *Free Culture: How Big Media Uses Technology and the Law to Lock Down Culture and Control Creativity.* New York, NY: Penguin Press, 2004.

Litman, Jessica. *Digital Copyright.* Amherst, NY: Prometheus Books, 2001.

Stallman, Richard. E-mail message posted to Unix-wizards and Usoft news-groups, September 27, 1983. Reprinted at GNU.org. Retrieved March 30, 2010 (http://www.gnu.org/gnu/initial-announcement.html).

Sun, Jeffrey C., and Benjamin Baez. *Intellectual Property in the Information Age: Knowledge as Commodity and Its Legal Implications for Higher Education*. Hoboken, NJ: Wiley, 2009.

Tallmo, Karl-Erik. "The Misunderstood Idea of Copyright." *Computer Sweden*, September 2005. Retrieved March 19, 2010 (http://www.nisus.se/archive/050902e.html).

Tallmo, Karl-Erik. "What Has Copyright to Do with Democracy?" *For or Against the Citizenry: Power-Sharing*. Djorke, Bo, et al., eds. Stockholm, Sweden: D2D, 2009.

Vaidhyanathan, Siva. *Copyrights and Copywrongs: The Rise of Intellectual Property and How It Threatens Creativity*. New York, NY: New York University Press, 2003.

INDEX

About the Author

Emily Popek is a writer and an editor at the *Daily Star* newspaper in Oneonta, New York, where she ensures her staff of reporters and photographers cite sources and respect copyrights in all instances.

Photo Credits

Designer: Nicole Russo; Photo Researcher: Cindy Reiman